Heart Sutra

Ancient Buddhist Wisdom in
the Light of Quantum Reality

Commentary by
Mu Soeng

Primary Point Press
Cumberland, Rhode Island

First edition, 1991
Second printing, 1992
Third printing, 1995

Cover calligraphy by Jakusho Kwong Roshi

Primary Point Press logo by Grazyna Perl, JDPSN

ISBN 0-942795-04-0

Exclusive trade distribution by
Atrium Publishers Group, Santa Rosa, California

Primary Point Press
99 Pound Road
Cumberland, RI 02864-2726
(401) 658-1476
Fax (401) 658-1188
Internet kwanumzen@aol.com

Acknowledgements

Many thanks to Zen Master Wu Kwang, Adria Evans, Sam Rose, Kathy Diehl and Richard Streitfeld for reading the manuscript and their valuable comments. Special thanks to J.W. Harrington for help with typesetting and production of this book.

Permissions:

Acknowledgement is made to the following for their kind permission to use materials from their publications:

Selections from *The Tao of Physics* © 1975 Frithjof Capra. Reprinted by permission of the publisher.

Selections from *The Silent Pulse* © 1978 George Leonard. Reprinted by permission of the author.

Selections from *Creative Meditation and Multi-Dimensional Consciousness* © 1976 Lama Angarika Govinda. Reprinted by permission of the publisher.

Selections from *The Buddhist Teaching of Totality* © 1971 The Pennsylvania State University Press. Reprinted by permission of the publisher.

Selections from *Ancient Wisdom and Modern Science* © 1984 State University of New York Press. Reprinted by permission of the publisher.

Selections from *The Heart of Understanding* © 1988 Thich Naht Hanh. Reprinted by permission of the publisher.

Introduction

At the heart of each of us, whatever our
imperfections, there exists a silent pulse of perfect
rhythm, a complex of wave forms and resonances,
which is absolutely individual and unique, and yet
which connects us to everything in the universe.
The act of getting in touch with this pulse can
transform our personal experience and in some
way alter the world around us.[1]

The convergence between science and
mysticism, between Eastern thought and
Western pragmatism, and the consequent
emergence of a new paradigm in recent times,
offers a renewed hope that we may yet be able
to transform ourselves and the world around us.
The dangers of failing to do so are readily
apparent, mostly in the near-destruction of the
ecological system of the planet. There are many
tools of transformation but the only place where
transformation really takes place is in the
human heart. The ancient traditions of the East
have always sought to understand the nature of
reality within one's own heart. It is not an

accident that the Chinese word *hsin* stands for Heart-Mind. In the Eastern way of looking at things, the thinking-feeling process is a unified field, in contrast to the Cartesian dualism of the western scientific mind. Human experience has shown that the heart-mind, being deeply conditioned, is not an easy place for conflicts to be resolved. This was brought out most vividly in the intense emotional and even existential crisis which the pioneers of quantum physics (the post-Einsteinian branch of physics that deals with the molecular structure of organisms at the subatomic level) underwent before they could accept the intellectual findings of their own experiments.

The *Heart Sutra,* an ancient scripture from the Mahayana wisdom schools of Buddhism, is an insight into the nature of ultimate reality through intuitive wisdom. The spaciousness of this insight allows the heart to beat in its naturalness, beyond disputations and ideological arguments. Now that quantum physics has found some very interesting parallels to the basic insights of the *Heart Sutra,* perhaps the intellectual and the intuitive can meet in the new paradigm. At the same time, while this commentary offers to view the insights of Mahayana Buddhism in the light of quantum physics, it carries no suggestion that the two are complementary or interchangeable.

They are, at best, two entirely different orders of reality, each reflecting completely different underlying processes that happen to converge. In his pioneering book, *The Tao of Physics,* Frithjof Capra has observed:

> The conception of physical things and phenomena as transient manifestations of an underlying fundamental entity is not only a basic element of quantum field theory, but also a basic element of the Eastern world view ... the intuition behind the physicist's interpretation of the subatomic world, in terms of the quantum field, is closely paralleled by that of the Eastern mystic who interprets his or her experience of the world in terms of an ultimate underlying reality.

> Buddhists express the same idea when they call the ultimate reality *Sunyata* — "Emptiness" or "the void"— and affirm that it is a living Void which gives birth to all forms in the phenomenal world .... Thus the Void of the Eastern mystic can easily be compared to the quantum field of subatomic physics. Like the quantum field, it gives birth to an infinite variety of forms which it sustains and, eventually, reabsorbs.[2]

The effort in this commentary is to see this convergence in a creative light, knowing fully well that after convergence the two orders of reality separate again and their underlying processes take a different turn. Above all, this commentary on the *Heart Sutra* is offered in the spirit of a Zen practitioner. This commentary arose out of my own need, and presumably the need of like-minded Zen students, to understand the historical and doctrinal background of this seminal document. At the same time, I wanted to be careful not to get caught in the minutiae of academic analysis and turn this commentary into yet another doctrinal point of view. In the present approach, the focus is not on doctrinal orthodoxy, but rather on creating a radical new understanding of an ancient teaching, and to understand this core teaching of Mahayana Buddhism in the light of new perspectives on reality and a new model of the universe set forth by quantum physics. Since the teaching of the *Heart Sutra* is centered around an insight into "emptiness," the Sanskrit word *sunyata* is used here throughout rather than its quite inadequate English translation. It is thus hoped that the inherent vibrancy of *sunyata* which has infused the spirit of Mahayana for the last two thousand years will emerge in the following commentary. Since the developed tradition of Zen bears the imprint of *sunyata* throughout, it is hoped as well that readers will approach this commentary through the prism of their meditation practice, and that the vibrancy of their practice will find resonance in the insights of the sutra. As Edward Conze has remarked,

> It cannot be the purpose of a commentary to convey directly to the reader the spiritual experiences which a sutra describes. They only reveal themselves to

persistent meditation. A commentary must be content to explain the words used.[3]

A note on the English translation of the sutra: There are many translations of the *Heart Sutra* now being used by various Zen communities in the United States. The translation used here is the one used by Kwan Um School of Zen and its member groups, with its head temple at Providence Zen Center.

The Heart Sutra

The Maha Prajna Paramita Hridaya Sutra

Avalokitesvara Bodhisattva when practicing deeply the Prajna Paramita perceives that all five skandhas are empty and is saved from all suffering and distress.

Sariputra, form does not differ from emptiness, emptiness does not differ from form. That which is form is emptiness, that which is emptiness form. The same is true of feelings, perceptions, impulses, consciousness.

Sariputra, all dharmas are marked with emptiness. They do not appear or disappear, are not tainted or pure, do not increase or decrease. Therefore, in emptiness, no form, no feelings, perceptions, impulses, consciousness. No eyes, no ears, no nose, no tongue, no body, no mind, no color, no sound, no smell, no taste, no touch, no object of mind, no realm of eyes and so forth until no realm of mind consciousness. No ignorance and also no extinction of it and so forth until no old age and death and also no extinction of them.

No suffering, no origination, no stopping, no path, no cognition, also no attainment with nothing to attain.

The Bodhisattva depends on Prajna Paramita and the mind is no hindrance. Without any hindrance, no fears exist. Far apart from any perverted views, one dwells in Nirvana.

In the three worlds, all Buddhas depend on Prajna Paramita and attain Anuttara Samyak Sambodhi.

Therefore, know that Prajna Paramita is the great transcendent mantra, is the great bright mantra, is the utmost mantra, is the supreme mantra which is able to relieve all suffering and is true not false. So proclaim the Prajna Paramita mantra, proclaim the mantra which says:

Gate, Gate, Paragate, Parasamgate, Bodhi Svaha.

Historical Background Of The Sutra

The term Buddhism, used generically and rather loosely, is best understood as an ever-evolving phenomenon with three distinct aspects to its history:

1) the original teachings of the historical person Siddhartha Gautama who became the Buddha, the Awakened One: the Four Noble Truths, including the Eightfold Path, and the Chain of Dependent Origination. There is a fair historical consensus on the authenticity of these teachings and the teacher;

2) the Buddhist Tradition, by which is meant the developed doctrines such as the Abhidharma canon of the Hinayana tradition, and the *sutras* (sermons attributed to the Buddha) and *sastras* (commentaries on the *sutras*) of the Mahayana tradition whose composition and compilation took place over a period of a thousand years after the death of the Buddha, and

3) the Buddhist Religion, which includes a smorgasbord of bewildering and seemingly contradictory practices and beliefs ranging from the marathoning monks of Mt. Hiei in Japan to the devotees of Pure Land and Nichiren sects in East Asia to the laity supporting the forest-monks in Thailand and Sri Lanka.

The *Heart Sutra,* or the "Prajnaparamita Hridaya Sutra," to give it its proper Sanskrit name, belongs to the Buddhist tradition, and is probably the best known of the Mahayana sutras. It is chanted daily in the Buddhist monasteries of China, Japan, Korea, Tibet and in the West. This very short sutra (containing about fourteen verses in Sanskrit and 260 characters in Chinese) is a basic text of Zen tradition and is considered to contain the essence of all Mahayana wisdom schools.

Zen (Ch'an) began in China as a meditation school of Mahayana Buddhism and was partially shaped by its *sutra* literature. These sutras capture the dramatic fervor and religious aspirations of new movements in India that had broken away from the earliest forms of Buddhism (Hinayana), beginning, most likely, in the first century BCE. The Mahayana doctrine developed, religiously and philosophically, with the Bodhisattva ideal (which exhorted a practitioner to work for the liberation of all beings, however numberless, rather than striving just for one's own liberation) at its center, and the teaching of *sunyatya* (Emptiness) as its inspiration. D.T. Suzuki, the great facilitator between Zen tradition and the West, finds, in the psychology of the Bodhisattva, "one of the greatest achievements in the life of the spirit."

Several of the schools of Mahayana Buddhism are based on a group of sutras known as Prajnaparamita Sutras or the Sutras of Transcendent Wisdom. The earliest portions of these sutras go back to the period 100 BCE. to 100 CE; the *Heart Sutra* itself has been dated by Edward Conze at 350 CE.

> The great Mahayana sutras form the center of Mahayana; in them the new religious inspiration is crystallized. A massive and imposing body of literature, the sutras differ greatly in content, but each and every one of them breathes the spirit of Mahayana. These widely scattered writings serve many religious communities. While individual sutras or groups of sutras take up particular themes, they concur and overlap at many points. Moreover, one and the same *sutra* can give rise to different religious movements. They are often accompanied by explanatory commentaries, or sastras.[4]

When Buddhism first moved from India to China in its Mahyana forms, it was known not as Buddhism but as the "Religion of Prajnaparamita" or, since the sutras of the Prajnaparamita centered around the teaching of *sunyata* (somewhat loosely translated as emptiness or nothingness), as the "Religion of Nothingness."

The *Heart Sutra* is one of approximately 38 sutras in the Prajnaparamita group, and its shortest. In it, the dynamic vibrancy of *sunyata* and the cryptic delineation of its meaning have been captured with a radical economy of expression that has exercised a fascination over the minds of countless generations of Buddhist thinkers in India, China, Tibet and other lands where Mahayana Buddhism flourished. Some of the greatest thinkers in Buddhist history, among them Atisa, Fa-tsang, Kukai, and Hakuin have written commentaries on the *Heart Sutra*.

While it celebrates *sunyata* as a timeless truth, the *Heart Sutra* has also to be seen as a historical document, engaged in rivalry with the rationalist-schematic approach taken by earliest sects of Buddhism (designated as "Hinayana" — the lower vehicle — by its rivals.) In the centuries after Buddha's death, the Hinayana followers, with the encyclopedic *Abhidharma* as their literature, had created categories of analysis to the point where it became, in the words of Heinrich Dumoulin, the Zen historian, "a dishearteningly lifeless product without metaphysical elan...." Mahayana sutras thunder again and again against philosophers (Abhidharmists) who are disposed to freeze reality into a categorical permanence and to discriminate between subject and object.

In the still-solidifying tradition of Mahayana, the *Heart Sutra* is a key document demolishing all these categories, and pointing out that all categories are ultimately dualistic and not leading to wisdom essential for enlightenment. In the earliest stages of the formation of Mahayana, there were schools of thought which proposed the doctrine of the "five words" of the Buddha; meditations on these words alone have transcendent significance and the power to bring liberation (which, they claimed, was not the case with the rest of his discourses.) These five words are: non-soul *(anatta)*, impermanence *(anicca)*, unhappiness *(dukkha)*, extinction *(nirvana)* and emptiness *(sunyata)*.

The first four of these words are shared by the early Mahayanists commonly with the Hinayanists; it is with the inclusion of *sunyata* (emptiness) as the last of these words that early Mahayana asserts its difference with the

Hinayana schools. For the Hinayanists, "emptiness" may be synonymous with the first word — non-self or non-soul — but its use was restricted in describing a person. Mahayana invention was not only to postulate *sunyata* (emptiness) as the essential emptiness of the phenomenal world, including the world within a person's mind; the thinkers of Mahayana took care to deny the existence of *sunyata* as yet another category. Thus we have the doctrine of *sunyata-sunyata,* the emptiness of emptiness. *Sunyata* is experienced as intuitive wisdom, and it is only through the intuitive wisdom of *sunyata,* the theme of Mahayana wisdom schools, that one is ferried across to the other shore of liberation.

The popularity of the *Heart Sutra* in the Buddhist tradition lies not only in its brevity but also in the elusiveness of its meaning. Distinguished commentators over the ages have discovered in it widely divergent interpretations which have led Edward Conze to observe that, "they tell us more what the text meant to them within their own culture than what the Indian original intended to convey."[5]

If that be the case, the divergent interpretations seem somehow quite appropriate since the elusive meaning of *sunyata* demands that each generation of Buddhist thinkers and practitioners in each culture come to grips with it through the praxis of their own experience.

The *Heart Sutra* has two versions, the longer and the shorter. The longer version has a prologue in which the Buddha enters into *samadhi* and an epilogue in which he rises from *samadhi* and praises the Bodhisattva Avalokitesvara. The shorter version, used here, begins without the prologue and has Avalokitesvara contemplating the meaning of the profound perfection of wisdom.

The Setting

The *Heart Sutra* is preached on Vulture Peak, east of the ancient Indian city of Rajagraha, the capital of the kingdom of Magadha. Rajagraha, along with Sravasti, was one of the two major cities of ancient India most frequently visited by the Buddha during his forty-five year teaching career. The Vulture Peak is said to have been a favorite site of the Buddha, and here he gave a number of sermons to assemblies of monks and laypeople.

The rather unique prologue (of the longer version) introduces us to the leading characters of the sutra: Shakyamuni Buddha, Avalokitesvara Bodhisattva and Sariputra. The Buddha does not speak in the prologue, but enters into samadhi and silently empowers Sariputra to ask and Avalokitesvara to answer. The silence of the Buddha here is characteristic of much of Mahayana literature, and supports its classical view that the Buddha is "no longer simply the teacher but is transformed into the principle of enlightenment, a silent, eternal, numinous presence, the *dharmakaya*."[6]

The *Heart Sutra* is the only Prajnaparamita text in which the Bodhisattva Avalokitesvara appears. His (or her) presence here is significant on several counts: first, it attests to the relatively late date of the sutra, a time when the cult of the Bodhisattva of Compassion, textually associated with the twenty-fourth chapter of the Lotus Sutra and the sutras of the Pure Land School, had become well-established. Secondly, the *Heart Sutra* is dedicated completely to the teaching of *sunyata* without any reference whatever to the other major theme of the Prajnaparamita sutras: compassion (which traditionally includes *upaya* or the Skillful Means of the *bodhisattva*.) The absence of this theme is countered, implicity, by the fact that the wisdom essential for the attainment of Buddhahood is proclaimed by a *bodhisattva* who is said to be the embodiment of compassion.

The presence of Sariputra is equally significant. The *Heart Sutra* does not inveigh against the Hinayana disciples of the Buddha, as is characteristic of the longer Mahayana sutras, in which the Hinayana disciples are considered inferior to the Bodhisattvas, both in their wisdom and in their aspiration to enlightenment. The presence of Sariputra here fulfills that function; Sariputra, in the Hinayana scriptures, is considered the wisest of the disciples of the Buddha, but here he comes across as perplexed and uninformed when asking Avalokitesvara how to practice the perfection of wisdom.

The Title: Maha Prajna Paramita Hridaya Sutra

Maha means great or large. *Prajna* means wisdom, more specifically intuitive wisdom. *Paramita* is commonly translated as "perfection" although, in a different etymological usage, it can also mean "that which has gone beyond" or "transcendent." *Hridaya* means "heart" but here, in the title of the sutra, it is used in the sense of a "core" or "essence" rather than a physical organ. *Sutra* is the spoken word; more specifically, in the Buddhist tradition, it is the sermon or the word spoken by the Buddha. Thus the full meaning of the title can be "the Great Heart of Perfect Wisdom" or "the Heart of Great Transcendent Wisdom." Or we may use poetic licence to translate it as "the Wisdom of the Great Heart of the Universe." That will certainly be in keeping with the insight offered by the sutra into *sunyata* as the core of the universe.

"Avalokitesvara Bodhisattva..."

Bodhi means being awake or enlightened; *sattva* means a living being, so *bodhisattva* means an awakened, enlightened being, a person who has diligently cultivated the qualities necessary to become a Buddha. Avalokitesvara is one of the celestial Bodhisattvas and an embodiment of compassion. In the Mahayana tradition, Avalokitesvara and Manjushri, who is the Bodhisattva of wisdom, represent the two core qualities — wisdom and compassion — necessary in the psychological life of a Bodhisattva.

"...when practicing deeply the Prajnaparamita..."

In the prologue of the longer version of the *sutra*, this line presents the Buddha as being immersed in deep *samadhi* while the *bodhisattva* Avalokitesvara too is absorbed in contemplating the meaning of the perfection of wisdom. The statement is significant here in that the tradition insists that "a looking into" the nature of reality is not a matter of mere intellectual analysis (which the followers of Mahayana at times accused the Hinayana Abhidharmists of doing) but demands deep absorption so that awareness moves from the merely superficial to the profoundly intuitive. This is true for the celestial *bodhisattva* as it is for each one of us. In the Mahayna cosmology, "Prajnaparamita" (the perfection of wisdom) is a goddess who has been called "the mother of the Buddhas"; her presence here can be interpreted either cosmologically or etymologically.

"...perceives that all five skandhas are empty..."

It is in this state of intuitive awareness that the *bodhisattva* perceives the five *skandhas* to be empty. Before we look at the term *skandhas,* it might be useful to deal first with the term "empty" since it is the central teaching, not only of the *Heart Sutra* but also of the entire Mahayana literature. A translation of the Sanskrit word *sunyata* into western languages has always been problematic. When translated as "void" or "emptiness," it has a nihilistic undertone, which is how the orientialists of the nineteenth century saw Buddhism and portrayed it accordingly. Fortunately our understanding of the term (and of Buddhism) has grown in recent decades and has outlasted the earlier malformed interpretations. Our current understanding of Buddhist meditative experiences has been greatly faciliated by the findings of quantum physics into the nature of ultimate reality; these findings have added a new dimension to our efforts to understand the meaning of the term *sunyata* and what it stands for.

For a very long time, the Newtonian/Cartesian scientific view of the world rested on the notion of solid, indestructible particles as the building blocks of matter and all life, moving in space and influencing each other by forces of gravitation and interacting according to fixed and unchangeable laws. This myth disintegrated under the impact of experimental and theoretical evidence produced by quantum physicists in the early decades of this century. The experiments of quantum physics showed that the atoms, the presumed fundamental building blocks of the universe, were, at their core, essentially empty. In experiments, subatomic particles showed the same paradoxical nature as light, manifesting either as particles or waves depending on how the experiment was set up. Quantum physicists, confronting the mysteries of the universe, were left facing Zen-like *koans* of their own: the sound of a quark, the shape of a resonance, the nature of strangeness!

Quantum physics has thus brought about a radical new understanding both of the particles and the void. In subatomic physics, mass is no longer seen as a material substance but is recognized as a form of energy. When a piece of seemingly solid matter — a rock or a human hand or the limb of a tree — is placed under a powerful electronic microscope:

the electron-scanning microscope, with the power to magnify several thousand times, takes us down into a realm that has the look of the sea about it... In the kingdom of corpuscles, there is transfiguration and there is samsara, the endless round of birth and death. Every passing second, some 2-1/2 million red cells are born; every second, the same number die. The typical cell lives about 110 days, then becomes tired and decrepit. There are no lingering deaths here, for when a cell loses its vital force, it somehow attracts the attention of macrophage.

As the magnification increases, the flesh does begin to dissolve. Muscle fiber now takes on a fully crystaline aspect. We can see that it is made of long, spiral molecules in orderly array. And all of these molecules are swaying like wheat in the wind, connected with one another and held in place by invisible waves that pulse many trillions of times a second.

What are the molecules made of? As we move closer, we see atoms, the tiny shadowy balls dancing around their fixed locations in the molecules, sometimes changing position with their partners in perfect rhythms. And now we focus on one of the atoms; its interior is lightly veiled by a cloud of electrons. We come closer, increasing the magnification. The shell dissolves and we look on the inside to find...nothing.

Somewhere within that emptiness, we know is a nucleus. We scan the space, and there it is, a tiny dot. At last, we have discovered something hard and solid, a reference point. But no! as we move closer to the nucleus, it too begins to dissolve. It too is nothing more than an oscillating field, waves of rhythm. Inside the nucleus are other organized fields: protons, neutrons, even smaller "particles." Each of these, upon our approach, also dissolve into pure rhythm.

These days they (the scientists) are looking for quarks, strange subatomic entities, having qualities which they describe with such words as upness, downness, charm, strangeness, truth, beauty, color, and flavor. But no matter. If we could get close enough to these wondrous quarks, they too would melt away. They too would have to give up all pretense of solidity. Even their speed and relationship would be unclear, leaving them only relationship and pattern of vibration.

Of what is the body made? It is made of emptiness and rhythm. At the ultimate heart of the body, at the heart of the world, there is no solidity. Once again, there is only the dance.

(At) the unimaginable heart of the atom, the
compact nucleus, we have found no solid object,
but rather a dynamic pattern of tightly confined
energy vibrating perhaps 10^{22} times a second: a
dance... The protons — the positively charged
knots in the pattern of the nucleus — are not only
powerful; they are very old. Along with the much
lighter electrons that spin and vibrate around the
outer regions of the atom, the protons constitute
the most ancient entities of matter in the universe,
going back to the first seconds after the birth of
space and time.[7]

It follows then that in the world of subatomic
physics there are no objects, only processes.
Atoms consist of particles and these particles
are not made of any solid material substance.
When we observe them under a microscope, we
never see any substance; we rather observe
dynamic patterns, continually changing into one
another — a continuous dance of energy. This
dance of energy, the underlying rhythm of the
universe, is again more intuited than seen. Jack
Kornfield, a contemporary teacher of
meditation, finds a parallel between the
behavior of subatomic particles and
meditational states:

When the mind becomes very silent, you can
clearly see that all that exists in the world are brief
moments of consciousness arising together with
the six sense objects. There is only sight and the
knowing of sight, sound and the knowing of sound,
smell, taste and the knowing of them, thoughts and

the knowing of thoughts. If you can make the mind very focused, as you can in meditation, you see that the whole world breaks down into these small events of sight and the knowing, sound and the knowing, thought and the knowing. No longer are these houses, cars, bodies or even oneself. All you see are particles of consciousness as experience. Yet you can go deep in meditation in another way and the mind becomes very still. You will see differently that consciousness is like waves, like a sea, an ocean. Now it is not particles but instead every sight and every sound is contained in this ocean of consciousness. From this perspective, there is no sense of particles at all.[8]

Energy, whether of wave or particle, is associated with activity, with dynamic change. Thus the core of the universe — whether we see it as the heart of the atom or our own consciousness — is not static but in a state of constant and dynamic change. This energy — now wave, now particle — infuses each and every form at the cellular level. No form exists without being infused by this universal energy; form and energy interpenetrate each other endlessly in an ever-changing dance of the molecules, creating our universe. This universal energy is itself a process, beyond the confines of time and space; a form, on the other hand, is an "event," existing momentarily in time and space. This "moment" may last for seventy or eighty years in the case of a human being, a thousand years in the case of a sequoia tree, a few million years in the case of a mountain, but internally, at the cellular level, each of these forms is in a process of change at any given moment. In the paradigms of quantum physics, there is ceaseless change at the core of the universe; in the paradigms of Mahayana wisdom, there too is ceaseless change at the core of our consciousness and of the universe.

But change implies change from something to something else. Without something to be changed, there would be no change. Without forms, there would be no change; without the energy of change, the forms would not be able to hold their balance and would collapse. In meditation practice, we see this dynamic, constant change in our own mind-body system.

It has been just as difficult for the human mind to accept the existence of *sunyata* at the core of the universe as it was for the early quantum physicists to accept the quantum randomness of the universe. Einstein had even hoped that the quantum theory he helped create was somehow flawed, hoping desperately, even in the face of the evidence of his own experiments, that there would be a hidden variable that would establish order in the quantum world. Later experiments, conducted at the University of California in Berkeley on Bell's theorem, confirmed the absence of any hidden variable, and showed that when either of two correlated particles were observed, no matter how far separated in space, the other was instantly affected by the observation — as if the two particles were embedded in the observing consciousness itself. Even before Bell's theorem, Werner Heisenberg, one of the founding fathers of quantum theory, formulated in his Uncertainty Principle that it is not possible to examine a situation or system without altering the system by the very act of examination; in the deepest experience of meditation, the object of consciousness is embedded in the observing consciousness; the two are fused together by the energy or *sunyata* out of which both emerge.

> A strange place is this world of the new physicists, a world of ultimate connectedness, where consciousness — or observership, as John Wheeler calls it — coexisted with the creation, and where it might be said that the vastness of space, the nuclear conflagration of starts, the explosions of galaxies are simply mechanisms for producing that first glimmer of awareness in your baby's eyes.[9]

Subatomic particles, then, are dynamic patterns, processes rather than objects. *Sunyata* too is a dynamic pattern rather than an entity. Henry Stapp, an atomic physicist, has remarked, "An elementary particle is not an independently existing unanalyzable entity. It is, in essence, a set of relationships that reach outward to other things."[10]

Compare this to Nagarjuna (100-200 CE, the great Buddhist thinker whose dialectic of Madhyamika — the Middle Way — sought to define the experience of Mahayana wisdom): "Things derive their being and nature by mutual dependence and are nothing in themselves."[11]

Some commentators on Nagarjuna's formulation of the Middle Way — between being and non-being, between realism and nihilism — have translated *sunyata* as "devoidness" rather than emptiness or nothingness. Nagarjuna's thesis holds that despite the absence of all substance, qualities, or essential characteristics in all existing things in this changing world, there does remain the ineffable, final reality which can be seen only with the eye of intuitive wisdom (*prajna*). A quantum physicist may contend that this Final Reality can be intuited at the other end of an electronic microscope!

Thus our understanding of the word *sunyata* becomes a bit more clear. All forms are momentary in time and space; while the form lasts, it has validity (which is different from reality), but this appearance is transitory and illusory. Therefore, a more appropriate and accessible way to understand *sunyata* may be to apprehend it as "momentariness" or "transitoriness" rather than emptiness. Ancient Buddhism recognized that all objects are fundamentally devoid of independent lasting substance (Sanskrit: *svabhava*). Instead the interplay of form and energy creates a transitory phenomenon which appears in time and space. Nagarjuna cautions us against the temptation to posit *sunyata* as a category and reminds us again and again that *sunyata* itself is empty (*sunyata-sunyata*). The only way to apprehend the dynamic nature of *sunyata* is through the transitory/momentary appearance of forms. If no forms were to be manifested through it, *sunyata* would be a dead, static mass but *sunyata's* function is to infuse the myriad forms. Thus, while *sunyata* itself is a process, the forms are a manifestation of that process and the process can be understood only through the momentary existence of the forms. It was in this sense of a dynamic, universal energy that ancient Mahayana Buddhism used the term *sunyata*.

In *The Tao of Physics*, Frithjof Capra makes a similar observation:

> The phenomenal manifestations of the mystical Void, like the subatomic particles, are not static and permanent, but dynamic and transitory,

coming into being vanishing in one ceaseless dance of movement and energy. Like the subatomic world of the physicist, the phenomenal world of the Eastern mystic is a world of *samsara* — of continuous birth and death. Being transient manifestations of the Void, the things in this world do not have any fundamental identity. This is especially emphasized in Buddhist philosophy which denies the existence of any material substance and also holds that the idea of a constant "self" undergoing successive experiences is an illusion.[12]

In Sanskrit, *sunya* means cipher or zero. In the West, a circle or a zero means nothingness. In Native American usage, a circle means coming together, a sharing. In Indian usage, a circle means totality, wholeness. As Garma C.C. Chang, the noted Buddhist scholar, has remarked,

Zero itself contains nothing, yet it cannot be held to be absolutely or nihilistically void. As a mathematical concept and symbol, zero has a great many functions and utilities, without which it would be practically impossible to execute business and scientific activities in this modern age. If someone asked you, "Is zero nothingness?" you would be hard pressed to give an appropriate reply. Zero is both nothing and the possibility of everything. It is definitely not something nihilistically empty, rather it is dynamic and vital to all manifestations. In the same way, *sunyata* does not mean complete nothingness; being "serenely vibrant," it has both negative and positive facets.[13]

In the same vein, Masao Abe, another noted contemporary Buddhist thinker, has remarked that for Nagarjuna emptiness was not non-being but "wondrous Being,"

> precisely because it is Emptiness which "empties" even emptiness, true Emptiness (Absolute Nothingness) is absolute Reality which makes all phenomena, all existents, truly be.[14]

Sunyata, then, carries and permeates all phenomena and makes their development possible. *Sunyata* is often equated with the absolute in Mahayana, since it is without duality and beyond empirical forms. In quantum physics, ultimate reality is equated with formless energy at the core of the atom. This energy (of physics) or *sunyata* (of Mahayana) is not a state of mere nothingness but is the very source of all life and the essence of all forms.

Another helpful way to undertand *sunyata* is through the Zen term of "nowness," sometimes used interchangeably with "momentariness." In the absence of a permanent, abiding substance anywhere, there is only the *nowness* of things: ephermeral, transitory, momentary. In traditional Buddhist literature, the "nowness" of things is described as *tathata* or "suchness." The concept of *tathata* was first formulated by Asvaghosha, another great Buddhist thinker who probably lived a hundred years before Nagarjuna, and influenced him greatly. In Asvaghosha's formulation, when the futility of all conceptual thinking is recognized, reality is experienced as pure "suchness." What is realized in suchness is the existence of form-as-itself (the treeness of the tree, for instance), but that realization is suffused in intuitive wisdom (*prajna*) so that the ultimate reality of the form is seen as momentary and essentially devoid (*sunya*) of any lasting substance. Masao Abe, among others, insists that "Emptiness is Suchness."

Lama Angarika Govinda uses the word "transparency" to come to a fuller understanding of *sunyata*:

If *sunyata* hints at the nonsubstantiality of the world and the interrelationship of all beings and things, then there can be no better word to describe its meaning than *transparency*. This word avoids the pitfalls of a pure negation and replaces the concepts of substance, resistance, impenetrability, limitation, and materiality with something that can be experienced and is closely related to the concepts of space and light.[15]

He goes on to elaborate,

Far from being the expression of a nihilistic philosophy which denies all reality, it (*sunyata*) is the logical consequence of the anatman (non-self) doctrine of nonsubstantiality. *Sunyata* is the emptiness of all conceptual designations and at the same time the recognition of a higher, incommensurable and indefinable reality, which can be experienced only in the state of perfect enlightenment.

While we are able to come to an understanding of relativity by way of reasoning, the experience of universality and completeness can be attained only when all conceptual thought, all word-thinking, has come to rest. The realization of the teachings of the Prajna-paramita Sutra can come about only on the path of meditative practice (*yogacara*), through a transformation of our consciousness. Meditation in this sense is, therefore, no more a search after intellectual solutions or an analysis of worldly phenomena with worldly means — which would merely be moving around in circles — but a breaking out from this circle, an abandoning of our thought-habits in order to "reach the other shore" (as it has been said not only in the *Prajna-paramita-hridaya,* but also in the ancient *Sutta Nipata* of the Pali Canon.) This requires a complete reverseal of our outlook, a complete spiritual transformation or, as the Lankavatara Sutra expresses it, "a turning about in the deepest seat of our consciousness." This reversal brings about a new spiritual outlook, similar to that which the Buddha experienced when returning from the Tree of Enlightenment. A new dimension of consciousness is being opened by this experience, which transcends the limits of mundane thought.[16]

"...five skandhas are..."

The Sanskrit word *skandha* literally means a group, a heap, or an aggregate. In Buddhist tradition, the five *skandhas* of form, feelings, perceptions, impulses and consciousness are taken to constitute the entirety of what is generally known as "personality." These four words ("five skandhas are empty") are the essence of the earliest Buddhist teachings. The Buddha taught the three marks of existence (suffering, non-self and impermanence) as the defining characteristics of individual human existence; to these three marks, the Mahayanists added the fourth mark of *sunyata* (emptiness) and extended the concept to each and any existent in the universe. A detailed look at the five *skandhas* will mean understanding the very basis of Buddhist teachings and will provide a solid foundation for an extended look into *sunyata*.

The first and the most obvious of the *skandhas* is the corporeal form (Sanskrit: *nama-rupa*) which comes into being as a result of the energies of four elements (earth, air, fire and water) coming together in a certain configuration; when looked at by quantum physics, a form is seen to be devoid of any solid, everlasting substance. The form is held together in time and space by the interacting energies of the four elements in a certain pattern and balance. The characteristics which all *skandhas*, whether physical or mental, share are: arising, stabilizing, decay and dissolution. Decay and dissolution occur when the balance in which the elements have been held together for a certain period of time loses its inner tension and the organism is left without the essential vitality to hold itself in time and space.

The *skandha* called feeling (Sanskrit: *vedana*) is the general concept for feelings and sensations. These feelings and sensations can be classified into pleasant, unpleasant and neutral. As with the *skandha* of corporeal form, feelings and sensations also arise as a result of certain factors coming together. They then gain an intensity, hold it for some time, lose the intensity after some more time, and finally disappear. A particular feeling or sensation may change into another feeling or sensation which, in turn, will go through the same process ad infinitum.

The *skandha* called perception (Sanskrit: *samjna)* includes perception of form, sound, smell, taste, touch and bodily impressions, and mental objects. Perception takes place only in relation to an object (or thought) and does not exist independently of an object of attention.

The *skandha* called impulse (Sanskrit: *samskara*) refers to mental formations. In *Abhidharma-pitaka*, the traditional compendium of Buddhist psychology, a total of fifty-two impulses are listed, and include mental activities such as volition, attention, discrimination, joy, happiness, equanimity, resolve, effort, compulsion, concentration, and so on; included in this *skandha* are all the volitional impulses or intentions that precede an action. Since actions can be either physical, verbal, or mental, impulses can accordingly be physical, verbal or mental. This *skandha* refers both to the activity of forming and the passive state of being formed. The impulses thus are the impressions, tendencies, and possibilities in one's consciousness, and are the sum total of one's character. The impulses are the result of the totality of one's actions and thoughts, including those of earlier births, and their continuing presence is the condition for a rebirth. If they are absent, no karma is produced and no further birth takes place. Since the impulses can be good, bad or neutral, they determine the type of rebirth that will take place since their quality conditions consciousness, and through them consciousness seeks a form in rebirth to manifest those qualities.

The *skandha* called consciousness (Sanskrit: *vijnana*) is the faculty of knowing. Consciousness is a reaction or response which has one of the six organs (of eyes, ears, nose, tongue, body and mind) as its basis and one of the six corresponding external phenomena (visual form, sound, smell, taste, touch and mental thoughts) as its object. Consciousness arises out of contact between the object and the corresponding organ, but consciousness does not recognize an object itself. It is only a sort of awareness, awareness of the presence of an object. For instance, when eye comes into contact with a blue color, eye-consciousness simply "sees" the presence of a color. The recognition that the color is blue comes from the *skandha* of perception, the third aggregate discussed above. Likewise, the hearing-consciousness only hears the sound but does not recognize the category of sound; this is done by the perception-aggregate, and so on.

A commonly-made mistake about consciousness is to misunderstand it as some sort of soul or permanent self or continuum that proceeds through one life and onto the next. The Buddha taught that consciousness arises only out of conditions; without the presence of conditions there is no consciousness. Consciousness depends on form, feelings, perceptions and impulses for its arising and cannot exist independently of them. It is essentially an observing function.

"...and is saved from all suffering and distress."

All suffering is caused by delusion — delusion as to the nature of ultimate reality. Ultimate reality, in Buddhist view, for which now some very interesting parallels have been provided by quantum physics, is neither being (particle) nor non-being (wave), neither solid nor abiding in space-time continuum. .The qualities of non-self (Sanskrit: *Anatman*) and impermanence (Sanskrit: *Anitya*) are the hallmark of each individual existence; it is only the ego which clings to the deluded view of a permanent self and distorts the nature of reality. In meditation, one apprehends on a direct, experiencial level that the five *skandhas* are mere processes and that no self exists in the sense of a permanent, eternal, integral, independent substance; it is through this apprehension that a person is saved from deluded views, and hence from pain and suffering that ensue from such deluded views.

"Sariputra, form does not differ from emptiness, emptiness does not differ from form. That which is form is emptiness, that which is emptiness form."

As noted above, like all phenomena, form is devoid of any inherent self-abiding nature. This devoidness (emptiness) is not a quality which a form gains in the course of its (momentary) existence but is infused with it from the very beginning. Quantum physics, as noted earlier, posits the energy of silent pulsation at the core of everything in the universe, thus defining for us emptiness or *sunyata* as the "core energy"; in this light it is possible to see all forms emerging out of this silent pulsation as in waves or particles at the cellular level.

The sutra insists that form is emptiness. There is a critical difference between form being empty and form being emptiness. *Sunyata*, in Prajnaparamita sutras, is the ultimate nature of reality; at the same time it does not exist apart from the phenomena but permeates each phenomenon. Therefore, *sunyata* cannot be sought apart from the totality of all forms. And, although all forms are qualified at their core by *sunyata,* its presence does not negate the conventional appearance of form. In this sense, emptiness is dependent upon the form it qualifies, as much as form is dependent on emptiness for its qualification. Thus form is emptiness, and emptiness is form. At its core level, form does not differ from emptiness nor does emptiness differ from form.

"The same is true of feelings, perceptions, impulses, consciousness."

In much as it does with form, the presence of emptiness does not negate the conventional appearance of feelings, perceptions, impulses, consciousness. All of these *skandhas* are constantly arising and dissolving as a result of certain conditions being present. These conditions are, in turn, empty and conditioned by another set of conditions which, too, are empty and so on, ad infinitum. All conditions qualifying other conditions qualifying the *skandhas* are momentary phenomena giving rise to momentary phenomena. None of these has any inherent self-nature.

"Sariputra, all dharmas are marked with emptiness."

Dharma is a comprehensive term with a variety of meanings and applications at multiple levels for both Hindus and Buddhists. In the sutra here, the term is used in the sense of a fundamental unit of existence, the building blocks of the empirical personality and its world. In this sense, the *dharmas* are something like the *atoms* of Democritus or the *monads* of Leibniz. The term "point-instant" comes closest perhaps to capturing the insight behind the term *dharma* within the context of the *Heart Sutra*. These "point-instants" have miniscule extension in space and have practically no endurance. Again, the analogy of wave-particle unpredictability best captures the drama of "point-instants."

It is out of these *dharmas*, the fundamental units, that the *skandhas* are made. Since all existence is manifested through one or another of the *skandhas,* it seems inevitable that all existence is a conglomeration of *dharmas*. But the *dharmas* themselves are not any solid objects positioned in time and space, just as the waves and particles of quantum physics are not. The *dharmas* make a momentary appearance and then flicker out. They appear as a result of the interplay of underlying *sunyata,* the core energy; hence they are inherently empty. There is absolutely nothing one can hold on to.

"They do not appear or disappear, are not tainted or pure, do not increase or decrease."

The quality of appearing or disappearing is usually attributed to (seemingly) solid objects. If the *dharmas* are seen as a series of momentary flickerings, they cannot be invested with having the quality of appearing or disappearing precisely because flickerings are not solid objects. A flickering, so swift in time and miniscule in space, is not, in itself, tainted or pure, nor does it increase or decrease. An appropriate analogy here is of the waves in the ocean. A large wave is not a solid entity by itself but is composed of a series of smaller waves which in turn are composed of still smaller waves and so on. Even while we get the illusion of a "wave," there is actually a remarkably swift movement of water in certain patterns. A wave does not exist out there in the ocean. Out of ignorance, we may attribute these qualities (of appearing/disappearing, taint/purity, increase/ decrease) to conventional appearances (*skandhas*) but, since at the core of conventional appearances, there are only unpredictable flickerings *(dharmas),* our acceptance of these qualities as real in themselves will be a deluded view. The only place where our deluded view will find resolution is in the reality of *sunyata.*

Also, the categories of arising and disappearing, pure and impure, increasing or decreasing, belong to the realm of affirmation and negation which are, in turn, produced by our conceptual thinking. In pure experience, there is no affirmation or negation. In the experience of *sunyata* there is only emptiness, not its affirmation or negation as having arisen or having disappeared, holy or unholy, etc. Here, it would be wise to remind ourselves of Nagarjuna's caution once again that as a concept *sunyata* too is empty. Any affirmation or negation of *sunyata* would be conceptual, and hence a deluded view.

"Therefore, in emptiness no form, no feelings, perceptions, impulses, consciousness. No eyes, no ears, no nose, no tongue, no body, no mind, no color, no sound, no smell, no taste, no touch, no object of mind, no realm of eyes and so forth until no realm of mind-consciousness."

This passage is a further triangulation of the earlier assertions by the Abhidharmists with regard to *skandhas* and *dharmas*. Not wishing the hearer to somehow form the misimpression that "emptiness is form," or any such category of analysis, the *sutra* now employs the classical Indian philosophical methodology of negation to rid the hearer of any such possibility. This methodology is two-pronged; on the one hand it denies any identification of emptiness with the *skandhas* (form, feelings, perceptions, impulses, consciousness) or the six sense-objects (eyes, ears, nose, tongue, body, mind) or the phenomena perceived by the six sense-organs (shape, sound, smell, taste, touch or thought) or the six consciounesses produced as a result of contact between the sense-organs and the external phenomena (eye consciousness, ear consciousness, nose consciousness, tongue consciousness, touch consciousness and mind consciounsess); in this sense, this negation is a rejection of the Hinayana predilection for numerous categories of analysis. On the other hand, the *sutra* asserts that *sunyata* is ineffable and inexpressible and is not to be confounded with eye, ear, nose, tongue, and so on, until any and all categories are denied as identifiable with *sunyata*.

Therefore, in *sunyata* there is nothing to hold on to. *Sunyata* is complete absence of all identifiable phenomena, yet it is not nihilistically void. What has ceased to operate in *sunyata* are all categories of analysis. When the rationality of the Hinayana thinking is transcended, and one enters into the realm of intuitive truth, only then does one experience the qualityless, valueless, ineffable *sunyata* of the Mahayana tradition.

"No ignorance and also no extinction of it and so forth until no old age and death and also no extinction of them."

This passage is a restatement of the insight contained in Buddha's enlightenment experience as well as a further negation of Hinayana rationality. The legend of Buddha's enlightenment tells us that in the first watch of the night of his great experience under the rose-apple tree, he experienced all his past lives, one by one, as he had lived them. In the second watch of the night, he witnessed the death and rebirth of all cosmos and all being in them, across the aeons. Still, to his credit, he was not satisfied that he had discovered the root cause of human suffering as he had set out to do when he took his great vow not to move from his seat under the tree. Finally, at dawn, he saw the Morning Star and, in a flash, understood what he had been seeking. This insight has been articulated in later tradition as the Chain of Dependent Origination (or the Chain of Causation) and presented as a schema:

1) there is ignorance (as to the true nature of reality);

2) ignorance leads to mental formations or impulses (the *skandha* called *samskara*);

3) impulses or mental formations give rise to consciousness (the *skandha* called *vijnana*), the totality of thoughts, speech and actions;

4) consciousness determines the resulting mental and physical phenomena (the *skandha* called *nama-rupa* or the realm of name and form);

5) mental and physical phenomena condition the six sense realms: the five physical sense-organs of eye, ear, nose, tongue, body, and the mind;

6) the six sense-realms come into contact with (sensorial and mental) phenomena;

7) contact gives rise to sensations or feelings (the *skandha* called *vedana*);

8) feelings give rise to desire or thirst;

9) thirst gives rise to clinging;

10) clinging gives rise to the process of becoming;

11) the process of becoming leads to rebirth;

12) rebirth leads to suffering, old age and death.

Often this Chain of Dependent Origination is graphically represented as a circle and variously called the Wheel of Samsara, the Wheel of Becoming or the Wheel of Karma. Through the preaching of his insights, the Buddha taught people how to turn the wheel in the reverse order — through the complete cessation of ignorance, mental formations are eradicated;

through the eradication of mental formations, consciousness is eradicated and so forth until one arrives at the cessation of conditioned rebirth and hence of suffering, old age, and death. This reverse turning is often called Turning the Wheel of Dharma and is called the path to *nirvana*, the state of being in which all deluded views as to anything in human personality being permanent or substantial are eradicated. It is important to bear in mind that each of the twelve factors in the Chain of Dependent Origination is conditioned as well as conditioning. As such, they are all interdependent and interconnected; in itself, no single factor is absolute or independent. Each factor is inherently empty. When the Wheel of Dharma is turned, all these factors find their resolution in *nirvana* or *sunyata*.

In sunyata, as noted earlier, forms are only flickerings — without any quality of solidity or time-endurance — manifesting themselves momentarily. Knowing this fundamental truth, we are spared the necessity of choosing one over the other, of attachment to one and aversion to another or both. Thus another occasion of clinging is dissolved. We are also spared the necessity to categorize the insight of the Buddha. Mahayana tradition insists that it is enough for a believer to firmly hold on to the thought of enlightenment and practice diligently. A firm belief that in *sunyata* all things find their resolution is therefore enough for a Mahayana believer. To know through the eye of wisdom that all the twelve links in the Chain of Dependent Origination are interconnections and inter-relations is to echo the words of Werner Heisenberg, one of the founders of quantum physics, "The world thus appears as a complicated issue of events, in which connections of different kinds alternate or overlap or combine and thereby determine the texture of the whole."[17]

"No suffering, no origination, no stopping, no path, no cognition, also no attainment with nothing to attain."

This is the most shocking rejection yet of the Hinayana approach to Buddha's teaching which had insisted that the totality of Buddha's teaching was contained in the first teaching he gave to his five former colleagues soon after his enlightenment. This teaching is called the First Sermon or the Sermon of the Four Holy Truths. In this schema, the four Noble Truths are:

1) existence is *dukkha* (pain, suffering, discomfort, dis-ease, sense of incompletion);

2) *dukkha* is caused by "thirst" (Sanskrit: *tanha*) — desire to be, desire to have;

3) the thirst can be stopped (*nirvana*);

4) it can be stopped by walking the eightfold path (namely — right understanding, right thoughts, right speech, right action, right livelihood, right effort, right mindfulness, right concentration).

The Mahayana disciples had no quarrel with the insight contained in any of these classifications but what precipitated a conflict for them was the Hinayana insistence on a monastic elitism which declared itself to be the sole custodian of Buddha's teachings and their interpretation. Through the innovation of *sunyata,* both as the ontological and transcendent nature of reality, the Mahayana followers declared all categories, and hence their interpretations, as dualistic, thus null and void. By positing a simple faith in the thought of enlightenment and diligent practice, they sought to make the Buddha's enlightenment experience available to any and all, laypersons and monastics alike.

This passage then is a declaration that suffering, origination of suffering, and the stopping of suffering by following a certain path are empty categories; at the same time, it is an affirmation that in the pure experience of *sunyata,* there are no dualities or distinctions between suffering and its stopping, between suffering and the so-called path to liberation. The *sutra* declares, almost ruthlessly, that there is no cognition or attainment with nothing to attain. Hinayana tradition had seen in the person of the *arhant* an embodiment of great spiritual attainment, and he was a model to be emulated. Historically, however, soon after the death of the Buddha, a controversy emerged over the status of the *arhant* and at the Second Council (held about a hundred years after the death of the Buddha); one of the key issues debated at the Council was whether or not it was possible for an *arhant* to relapse. The consensus, controversial though it was, was that an *arhant* can indeed relapse. Subsequent Mahayana literature built upon this limited capacity of the *arhant* and extended its belief system to include the transience of all categories of existence, including suffering, its cessation, and any attainment to come out of such cessation.

"The Bodhisattva depends on Prajnaparamita and the mind is no hindrance. Without any hindrance, no fears exists. Far apart from any perverted view, one dwells in Nirvana."

The *bodhisattva* is steadfast in his/her trust in the wisdom of *sunyata* and finds in it a sense of completion; he or she is completely at peace with it and with himself. This is his (her) support, and he knows there is nothing lacking in it. Whatever the limitations of his or her conditioned mind may be, he or she has a perfect understanding of, and trust in, the truth of *sunyata*. No perverted or deluded views are going to cloud his or her vision. In traditional Buddhism, there are "four perverted views" from which liberation is sought:

1) a view that anything existent can be permanent even if it is compounded;

2) a view that satisfaction may be found in the world of compounded entities;

3) a view that there is a permanent self or soul; and

4) a view that things are desirable and
    therefore worth striving for and clinging
    to.

An investment in any of these "perverted"
views is likely to produce fear and confusion.
Fear and confusion, by their very nature, seek
other things to cling to, and each clinging brings
about its own particular perverted view to
further cloud the vision. Rooted firmly in the
wisdom of *sunyata*, the *bodhisattva* has no such
hindrance. S/he does not mistake the unreal for
the real, the conditioned for the unconditioned,
the relative for the absolute, etc.

For a contemporary reader of the sutra, the
words, "no fears exist" may be the most
significant insight contained in the sutra. Our
century has been characterized by existential
angst and its concomitant despair and
hopelessness. The late twentieth century culture
finds itself driven by the basic fuel of fear even
while the individual is really yearning for love.
Our conditioning has become such that we fear
fear and we fear love. Any resolution of the
individual human condition has to perforce deal
with the basic fear of duality, fear of the
"other," fear of the world which one finds to be
hostile and threatening, and yet indispensable.
Unless this dichotomy, this sense of separation

from the world is resolved, all our efforts to find a "meaning" in human life are going to be nothing more than manipulative gestures. It is only in the pure experience of *sunyata* that one transcends the manipulative gestures which societal conditioning, in its ignorance, sees not as illusions but as substantive. The training of the *bodhisattiva* is to see the illusory nature of these manipulative gestures and transcend them.

Without a clouded vision, the *bodhisattva* "dwells in *nirvana*." For the earlier Hinayana, *nirvana* was the state of liberation resulting from the eradication of suffering caused by desires and any notion of a permanent selfhood. As happened with many other aspects of Buddha's teaching, *nirvana* too came to be posited as a category in the Abhidharma scheme of things. Mahayana response to this position was that while the Hinayana follower had certainly achieved a measure of peace, his understanding of liberation was limited as long as he persisted in having a fear of *samsara* (the world of desires and becoming) and felt that *samsara* had to be overcome by attaining *nirvana*. This is a dualistic approach and, according to Mahayana, cannot lead to the Transcendent Wisdom which is essentially non-dualistic and in which *samsara* and *nirvana* are not distinct from each other. *Nirvana* is not to be considered as "something," a category, which exists as a separate reality apart from everything else; *nirvana* is not the result of doing something or attaining something but of not-doing: the not-doing of not discriminating. The *bodhisattva* does not "attain" *nirvana* (since any attainment is empty of time-endurance or self-nature) but having the unclouded vision of non-discrimination, in other words, of *sunyata*, he is always immersed in tranquility and is at peace with himself or herself. *Nirvana* is *sunyata* and *sunyata* itself is nirvana. *Nirvana* is *sunyata* because it has no graspable nature; any thought of *nirvana* as an attainable object would therefore be an error. *Nirvana* is not something to be striven for but to be intuited in the unfolding of each moment where *sunyata* plays itself out unceasingly. Through his intuitive wisdom (*prajna*), the *bodhisattva* knows that in *sunyata* all things are just as they really are i.e. full of Thusness or Suchness (Sanskrit: *Tathatha*).

"In the three worlds all Buddhas depend on Prajnaparamita and attain Anuttara Samyak Sambodhi."

The "three worlds" are the worlds of past, present and future (sometimes also referred to as the worlds of form, formlessness, and desire.) The vehicle through which the Buddhas attain their Buddhahood is the Transcendent Wisdom of *sunyata*.

Anuttara Samyak Sambhodi means "Perfect Unexcelled Awakening." It is the enlightenment of a perfect Buddha, one who has by himself rediscovered the teaching that leads to liberation. *Anuttara Samyak Sambodhi* also means possession of the "ten powers" (Sanskrit: *Dashabala)* of a perfect Buddha:

1) knowledge of discernment in any situation of what's possible and what's not;

2) knowledge of ripening of deeds in oneself and others;

3) knowledge of superior and inferior abilities of other beings;

4) knowledge of tendencies in other beings;

5) knowledge of the manifold constituents of the world;

6) knowledge of paths leading to rebirth in various realms of existence;

7) knowledge of what will lead to purity and what to impurity;

8) knowledge of various meditations (*dhyana*) and concentrations (*samadhi*);

9) knowledge of death and rebirth;

10) knowledge of when the defilements are completely eradicated.

The "attainment" of these ten powers in *Anuttara Samyak Sambodhi* may seem, on the surface, a logical contradiction since the sutra has just declared that there is "no attainment, with nothing to attain." The implicit message here is that in and of itself *Anuttara Samyak Sambodhi* too is empty but the ten powers arising out of deep contemplation on the wisdom of *sunyata* can be used as "skillful means" (Sanskrit: *upaya*) which, along with wisdom and compassion, are the hallmark of a *bodhisattva* in the Mahayana literature. Having these ten powers at his or her disposal, the *bodhisattva* works tirelessly to save all beings, knowing fully well that all is inherently empty. The effort is directed toward helping individuals change their karmic legacies and patterns rather than "saving" any solidity called "being."

Anuttara Samyak Sambodhi changes the complexion of the sutra from a mere negation of Hinayana categories to a positive fullfillment of the *bodhisattva* vow ("Sentient beings are numberless; I vow to save them all.") The *bodhisattva* treads on this path immersed in the intuitive wisdom of *sunyata* rather than the rational categories of the Hinayana model or having the illusion that there is someone who can "save" someone. The wisdom of *sunyata* is not an opinion or a category but an experience; it is an experience in which *"sunyata* is" rather than *"sunyata* is something." The experiencer and the experienced are inseparable, indistinguishable from each other. The *bodhisattva* and those he or she is trying to "save" are inseparable from each other.

In the sense of celebrating the insight into *sunyata*, the sutra ends here. Historically, however, by the time the *Heart Sutra* was given its final shape, the influence of Mantrayana (the vehicle of *mantra* practice) and Tantra was clearly ascendent within Mahayana. The following passage is to be seen, therefore, in historical context as an addendum and proselytizing in nature. The assertions made here clearly contradict the insights presented earlier in the sutra. Commentators through the ages have taken opposite positions on the inclusion of the *mantra* in the *sutra*; perhaps the best way to sum up the place of the *mantra* in the *sutra* is to note the historical context and leave it entirely up to the reader — to use this mantra as an incantation, as a tool of power; a more discerning inquirer may see the *mantra* as a linguistic and symbolic summation of the central teaching of the Mahayana wisdom schools.

A very positive view of this mantra is offered by Thich Naht Hanh, the contemporary Vietnamese Zen master:

> When we listen to this mantra, we should bring ourselves into that state of attention, of concentration, so that we can receive the strength emanated by Avalokitesvara Bodhisattva. We do not recite the *Heart Sutra* like singing a song, or with our intellect alone. If you practice the meditation on emptiness, if you penetrate the nature of interbeing with all your heart, your body, and your mind, you will realize a state that is quite concentrated. If you say the mantra then, with all your being, the mantra will have power and you will be able to have real communication, real communion with Avalokitesvara, and you will be able to transform yourself in the direction of

enlightenment. This text is not just for chanting, or to be put on an altar for worship. It is given to us as a tool to work for our liberation, for the liberation of all beings.[18]

"**Therefore, know that Pranjaparamita is the great transcendent mantra, is the great bright mantra, is the utmost mantra, is the supreme mantra which is able to relieve all suffering and is true, not false.**"

Clearly this message is intended for the unconvinced and the uninitiated. It asks for faith and trust in the efficacy of the *sutra* (which was the hallmark of Mahayana methods of veneration) rather than the critical-analytical faculty of self-investigation which Hinayana demanded from its followers. A faith in the power of a *mantra* is a further development in Mahayana and complementary to the growing popularity of the Lotus (*Saddharam-pundarika*) Sutra and other sutras from the Pure Land School; this trend in Mahayana would give rise to Tantra and become all-dominant in Buddhist cultures in Tibet, China, Japan and Korea where missionaries from India made remarkable gains in the course of their religious adventure treks.

The magico-mantrik culture which these missionaries brought with them found receptive soil in the countries of north and east Asia and led to tremendous religious-social-cultural realignments in these lands.

"So proclaim the Prajnaparamita mantra, proclaim the mantra which says:

"Gate, Gate, Paragate, Parasamgate, Bodhi Svaha."

Gate, gate means gone, gone; *paragate* means gone over; *parasamgate* means gone beyond (to the other shore of suffering or the bondage of *samsara*); *bodhi* means the Awakened Mind; *svaha* is the Sanskrit word for homage or proclaimation. So, the *mantra* means "Homage to the Awakened Mind which has gone over to the other shore (of suffering)."

Whatever perspective one may take on the inclusion of the *mantra* at the end of the *sutra*, it does not put a blemish on what the *sutra* has tried to convey earlier: the richness of intuitive wisdom coming out of the pure experience of complete stillness, of complete cessation, away from all concepts and categories.

Zen masters, in echoing the theme of emptiness, like to agree with existentialist thinkers that "life" has no meaning or reason. The *Heart Sutra* uses the methodology of negation as a way of pointing to this lack of any inherent meaning or reason in the phenomenal world, including the world of the mind. It takes each of the existents, holds it up under an unflinching gaze and declares it to have no sustaining self-nature. This is the wisdom teaching of *sunyata* of the Mahayana tradition. But, at the same time, compassion is the other and equally important teaching of Mahayana. How do we then bridge the gap between *sunyata* as ultimate reality and the conventionality of human condition? The existentialist thinkers agonized over this problem and were led to despair and anarchy. In Mahayana, compassion, which is a natural, unforced by-product of a deep state of meditation, supports the wisdom of emptiness, yet allows the individual to have empathy with the conventional appearance of the world without getting lost in it. It may be that compassion works best as a post-enlightenment existential crisis, but nontheless without compassion as a guiding paradigm, the unrelenting precision of *sunyata* can make life unbearable.

Zen masters insist that our true freedom lies in the choices we make, and each one of us has the power to change "no meaning" into Great

Meaning, "no reason" into Great Reason. This is possible because in the pure experience of *sunyata,* one realizes that one is intrinsically endowed with Buddha-nature and that this Buddha-nature in oneself is not different from Buddha-nature in all living beings. To see others as separate from oneself is to live in delusion and deny one's own Buddha-nature; to see others as sharing in one's own Buddha-nature is to affirm one's essential humanity. In making the free choice of compassion for all beings, we are doing no more than giving expression to our own Buddha-nature. It is only in compassion (Sanskrit: *karuna)* that wisdom (*prajna)* finds its fullest expression.

Graphically, this way of understanding the *Heart Sutra* in the Zen and Mahayana traditions may be presented as a circle:

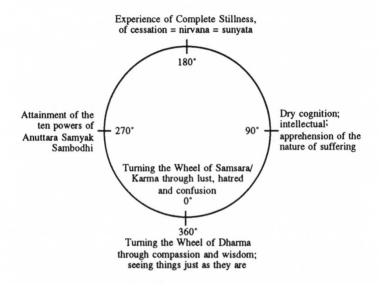

At **0 degree** is *samsara*. Here the Wheel of Karma keeps turning on and on, fueled by anger, greed and ignorance. An urgency to change, to get out of the realm of suffering leads one to

90 degrees. Here one has an intellectual awareness of the Four Noble Truths and the Chain of Dependent Origination in the Hinayana-Abhidharma sense, but this is dry cognition. When one follows this dry cognition with a deep experience of meditation samadhi, one reaches the experience of

180 degrees. This is the experience of Complete Stillness, of *sunyata,* of cessation. Here the mind becomes completely silent and personal and societal conditioning disappears. In Zen terms, this is the realization of Buddha-Nature. A thorough absorption in this samadhi leads to

270 degrees where one acquires the ten powers of *Anuttara Samyak Sambodhi.* This is the attainment of Buddhahood in traditional Buddhist sense. At the same time one understands from one's wisdom-eye that in themselves these powers too are empty; this wisdom leads one to

360 degrees. This is *nirvana* in action, Buddhahood manifested in functioning in the world. Here the Wheel of Dharma is turned by employing skillful means (*upaya*), rooted in wisdom and compassion. Here one finds validation of one's *bodhisattva* vows, which is a continuation of what Shakyamuni Buddha did in his forty-five years' teaching career.

More than two centuries ago, Voltaire wrote, "Man makes his own gods, forges forever new chains for himself." Today, we live in a post-religious society; our psychological and spiritual needs have transcended the making of gods and forging of new chains for ourselves. Our need today is to find a new paradigm in which the intellectual and the intuitive meet, a paradigm which is rooted in the wisdom of our own meditative experience. Today, researchers in the field of consciousness use terms like "holographic" to describe a new model of the universe in which an individual is a "hologram" and exists in a state of "holonomy" in the so-called "holographic" universe.

The idea of the universe as an overachieving unity repeated somehow in each of its parts bears a majesty and elegance all its own....The holonomic formulation...resonates with one of the most ancient intuitions of the race, expressed with eloquence and force in Eastern philosophy. It helps account for the essential meaningfulness of existence, the coherent, repeated patterns that we keep discovering at the deepest structure of language, mathematics, and the physical world. It is a necessary consequence of modern quantum theory taken to its logical extreme.[19]

The "holographic" model of the universe cannot be replicated in individuals by turning it into yet another ideology for societal realignment. Without an experience of *sunyata,* which allows us to get in touch with our basic humanity, it will be just another concept, subject to disputations and dissertations. But if we are wise enough to learn from the experience of Mahayana mystics and the findings of quantum theory, we can find that:

A world of connectedness, potential, and evolution turns us toward a vivid sense of community along with the acceptance of personal responsibility; toward a de-emphasis on competing and winning along with a re-emphasis on participating and experiencing; from aggression toward gentleness and enjoyment; from dominance of nature to blending with nature; from exponential growth in production and consumption to a more moderate, more ecological standard of living along with a powerful intentionality; toward social justice throughout the world.[20]

Compare this to the sentiments echoed by a contemporary Zen master in the context of the *Heart Sutra:*

The Prajnaparamita gives us a solid ground to making peace with ourselves, for transcending the fear of birth and death, the duality of this and that. In the light of emptiness, everything is everything else, we inter-are, everyone is responsible for everything that happens in life. When you produce peace and happiness in yourself, you begin to realize peace for the whole world. With the smile that you produce in yourself, with the conscious breathing you establish within yourself, you begin to work for peace in the world. To smile is not to smile only for yourself; the world will change because of your smile. When you practice sitting meditation, if you enjoy even one moment of your sitting, if you establish serenity and happiness inside yourself, you provide the world with a solid base of peace. If you do not give yourself peace, how can you share it with others? [21]

References

[1]Leonard, George, *The Silent Pulse*, p.xii.

[2]Capra, Frithjof, The Tao of Physics, pp.197-98.

[3]Conze, Edward, *Buddhist Wisdom Books*, p.18.

[4]Dumoulin, Heinrich., *Zen Buddhism, A History,* Vol.1, p. 35.

[5]Conze, Edward quoted by Donald Lopez, Jr. in *The Heart Sutra Explained,* p. 3.

[6]Lopez, Donald, Jr., *The Heart Sutra Explained*, p.7.

[7]Leonard, George, *The Silent Pulse,* pp.32-34.

[8]Kornfield, Jack, "The Smile of the Buddha," *Ancient Wisdom and Modern Science,* p.101.

[9]Leonard, George, *The Silent Pulse*, p.176.

[10]Capra, Frithjof, "The New Vision of Reality," *Ancient Wisdom and Modern Science,* p.138.

[11]Ibid, p.138.

[12]Capra, Frithjof. *Tao of Physics,* pp.198-99.

[13]Chang, Garma C.C., *Buddhist Teaching of Totality,* pp.60-61.

[14]Abe, Masao, *Zen and Western Thought,* p. 94.

[15]Govinda, Lama Angarika, *Creative Meditation and Multi-Dimensional Consciousness,* p.11.

[16]Ibid, pp. 60-61.

[17]Heisenberg Werner, quoted by Frithjof Capra, "The New Vision of Reality," *Ancient Wisdom and Modern Science,* p. 137.

[18]Hanh, Thich Naht, *The Heart of Understanding,* pp. 50-51.

[19]Leonard, George, *The Silent Pulse,* p.89.

[20]Ibid, p.177.

[21]Hanh, Thich Naht, *The Heart of Understanding,* pp.51-52.

Bibliography

Abe, Masao. *Zen and Western Thought.* Honolulu: University of Hawaii Press, 1985.

Capra, Frithjof. *Tao of Physics.* Boston: Shambala, 1976.

— "The New Vision of Reality: Toward a synthesis of Eastern Wisdom and Modern Science" in *Ancient Wisdom and Modern Science.* Albany: State University of New York Press, 1984.

Chang, Garma C.C. *Buddhist Teaching of Totality.* University Park: Pennsylvania State University Press, 1971.

Conze, Edward. *Buddhism: Its essence and development.* New York: Harper and Row, 1975.

—*Buddhist Thought in India.* Ann Arbor: University of Michigan Press, 1967.

—*Buddhist Wisdom Books.* New York: Harper and Row, 1972.

—*Selected Sayings from the Perfection of Wisdom.* Boulder: Prajna Press, 1978.

—*Thirty Years of Buddhist Studies.* Columbia: University of South Carolina Press, 1968.

Dumoulin, Heinrich. *Zen Buddhism: A History (Vol.1).* New York: Macmillian Publishing Co. 1988.

Fox, Douglas A. *The Heart of Buddhist Wisdom.* Lewiston, N.Y: Edwin Mellen Press, 1985.

Govinda, Lama Angarika. *Creative Meditation and Multi-Dimensional Consciousness.* Wheation, IL: Theosophical Publishing House, 1976.

Hanh, Thich Naht. *The Heart of Understanding.* Berkeley: Parallax Press, 1988.

Kenney, Jim. "Particle, Wave, and Paradox" in *Fireball and the Lotus,* edited by Ron Miller and Jim Kenney. Santa Fe: Bear & Company, 1987.

Kornfield, Jack. "The Smile of the Buddha: Paradigms in Perspective" in *Ancient Wisdom and Modern Science,* edited by Stanislav Graf. Albany: State University of New York Press, 1984.

Kothari, D.S. "Atom and the Self" in *The Evolution of Consciousness,* edited by Kishore Gandhi. New York: Paragon House, 1983.

Leonard, George. *The Silent Pulse.* New York: E.P. Dutton, 1978.

Lopez, Donald S. *The Heart Sutra Explained.* Albany: State University of New York Press, 1988.

Murti, T.R.V. *The Central Philosophy of Buddhism.* London: George Allen & Unwin Ltd. 1955.

Streng, Frederick. *Emptiness: A Study in Religious Meaning.* Nashville: Abingdon Press, 1977.

Talbot, Michael. *Mysticism and the New Physics.* New York: Bantam Books, 1980.

Wallace, Alan B. *Choosing Reality: A contemplative view of Physics and the Mind.* Boston: Shambala, 1989.

Primary Point Press is the publications division of the Kwan Um School of Zen. It has published *Gathering of Spirit: Women Teaching in American Buddhism*, edited by Ellen Sidor (1987) and *Ten Gates: The Kongan Teaching of Zen Master Seung Sahn* (1987). It has reprinted *Only Don't Know: The Teaching Letters of Zen Master Seung Sahn* (1982); *Thousand Peaks: Korean Zen — Tradition and Teachers* by Mu Soeng Sunim (1987); and *Bone of Space: Poems by Zen Master Seung Sahn* (1982).

The Kwan Um School of Zen is a network of centers under the spiritual direction of Zen Master Seung Sahn and senior teachers. The school publishes Primary Point, an international journal of Buddhism. More information about the Kwan Um School of Zen, including a list of centers worldwide, may be received by contacting the school at:

99 Pound Road
Cumberland, Rhode Island 02864-2726
Telephone (401) 658-1476
Fax (401) 658-1188
Internet kwanumzen@aol.com